A

philosophy 'anthroposophy', meaning 'wisdom of the human being'. As a highly developed seer, he based his work on direct knowledge and perception of spiritual dimensions. He initiated a modern and universal 'science of spirit', accessible to anyone willing to exercise clear and unprejudiced thinking.

From his spiritual investigations Steiner provided suggestions for the renewal of many activities, including education (both general and special), agriculture, medicine, economics, architecture, science, philosophy, religion and the arts. Today there are thousands of schools, clinics, farms and other organizations involved in practical work based on his principles. His many published works feature his research into the spiritual nature of the human being, the evolution of the world and humanity, and methods of personal development. Steiner wrote some 30 books and delivered over 6000 lectures across Europe. In 1924 he founded the General Anthroposophical Society, which today has branches throughout the world.

THE SECOND
COMING OF CHRIST

RUDOLF STEINER

Sophia Books

Sophia Books
An imprint of Rudolf Steiner Press
Hillside House, The Square
Forest Row RH18 5ES

www.rudolfsteinerpress.com

Published by Rudolf Steiner Press 2008

First published in a translation by D. S. Osmond and C. Davy
by Anthroposophical Publishing Co. in 1961

This translation revised by Matthew Barton
© Rudolf Steiner Press 2008

Originally published in German as part of the volume entitled
Das Ereignis der Christus-Erscheinung in der ätherischen Welt
(volume 118 in the *Rudolf Steiner Gesamtausgabe* or Collected
Works) by Rudolf Steiner Verlag, Dornach. This authorized
translation is published by permission of the Rudolf Steiner
Nachlassverwaltung, Dornach

A catalogue record for this book is available from the British
Library

ISBN 978 185584 207 6

Cover by Andrew Morgan
Typeset by DP Photosetting, Neath, West Glamorgan
Printed and bound in Great Britain by Cromwell Press Limited,
Trowbridge, Wiltshire

Contents

When someone engages for a time with the view of the world that spiritual science offers, allowing the various ideas, thoughts and insights he gains from it to work upon him, a great many questions arise. He becomes a spiritual scientist himself to the degree he connects such questions—which are really those of feeling, of the heart, of the character, in fact of life in general—with ideas derived from the science of the spirit. By their very nature these ideas do not merely satisfy our theoretical or academic curiosity, but rather shed light on life's riddles, on the mysteries of existence. And they bear fruit in a real sense only when we no longer merely reflect on and feel their significance, value and meaning but also, through their influence, learn to look differently at the world around us. These ideas should inwardly warm us, should become impetus for our lives, and forces of heart and soul. Increasingly this is so when the answers we find to certain questions give rise to new questions, and when answers to these in turn become questions followed by new answers, and so on. By this means we can make progress both in spiritual knowledge and in the life of spirit.

Although some time will have to pass before the more intimate aspects of spiritual life can be aired in public lectures, the time should be near at hand for doing so within our own groups. It is inevitable that new members may be taken aback or even shocked when they hear certain things, but we must take this in our stride since we cannot progress in our work without illuminating more sensitive issues through spiritual-scientific investigation and knowledge. Therefore—although misunderstandings may arise in those of you who have engaged in spiritual life for a comparatively short time only—we will today again consider some of these more intimate insights of spiritual knowledge.

There is no doubt that an earnest question will rise in us when we think about the idea of reincarnation, of many earth lives—not merely as abstract theory but when we ponder deeply on the meaning and implications of this spiritual fact. The significant answer that reincarnation gives us will be followed by new questions. We may ask, for instance, what the deeper meaning is of the fact that we live many times on earth, returning again and again in new incarnations. The usual answer is that by passing through many repeated lives we ascend ever higher, experiencing the fruits and results of former lives on earth in subsequent ones, and thus progressing and developing. But that is still a rather general, abstract answer. It is only through more precise knowledge of the whole purpose of life on earth that we can fathom the significance of repeating incarnations.

If we kept returning to an earth that never changed but essentially remained the same, there would be little to learn from successive incarnations. These incarnations are important because, as we pass through each one, we can learn new things and have new experiences on earth. This is not so clearly perceptible over short periods, but if we survey long periods, as the science of the spirit enables us to do, it becomes evident that each epoch of our earth differs substantially from another in character, and that we thus undergo new and different experiences. But we have to realize something else too, taking these changes in the life of the earth into account: if in a particular epoch we neglect the opportunity to experience and learn what that epoch has to offer, then although we return in a new incarnation we have missed something, have failed to assimilate what we should have done in a previous epoch. In the next epoch, therefore, this means we are unable to make proper use of our forces and faculties.

Speaking still in quite a general sense, we can say that in our epoch something is now possible on earth, indeed almost everywhere on the globe, that was not possible in the former incarnation of those now alive. Strange as it may seem there is a certain and indeed great significance in this. In their present incarnation it is possible for certain numbers of people to find their way to spiritual science—that is, to absorb and integrate the findings of spiritual investigation available today in the field of spiritual science. It may of course be regarded as unimportant that a few people gather and acquire the knowledge made available by spiritual investigation; but people who think this fail to understand the importance of reincarnation or that certain things can be learned only during one particular incarnation. If they are not learned, something has been missed and will be lacking in subsequent incarnations.

Above all we should realize that what we learn today in spiritual science is incorporated into our soul, and we bring it with us when we descend again to a new incarnation.

Let us now try to grasp what this means for the soul. I will need to refer not only to much with which you are already familiar from other lectures, and from your own reading, but also to many spiritual realities that are more or less new or even quite unfamiliar to you. We must first look back, as we often have done, to earlier epochs in the evolution of humanity and the earth. We are living now in the fifth epoch after the great Atlantean catastrophe. This epoch was preceded by the fourth, the Graeco-Roman epoch, when the ideas and experiences that were of paramount importance on earth at the time originated among the Greek and Roman peoples. Before this epoch came the period focused on Chaldea, Babylonia, Assyria and Egypt; before that came the ancient Persian civilization, and prior to that the culture of ancient India. In a still more distant past we come to the great Atlantean catastrophe, when an ancient continent extending over the area of the present Atlantic Ocean was destroyed. This continent of ancient Atlantis was gradually submerged, and the solid earth on which we are now living acquired its present configuration. In still earlier epochs preceding the Atlantean catastrophe, we come to the civilizations and forms of culture developed on Atlantis by the Atlantean races, which in turn were preceded by still older cultures.

What historical records tell us—and these, after all, do not go back very far—may easily suggest that conditions on the earth were always the same as they are today. In fact this is quite unfounded, even for more recent eras. There have in fact been fundamental changes, most marked in the human soul and consciousness. The souls of those sitting here today were incarnated in bodies at all these different periods of the earth's evolution, and during each they absorbed what was possible at that time. In each successive incarnation the soul develops different faculties. Although the difference was perhaps less radical during the Graeco-Roman epoch, in ancient Persian culture, and even more so in that of ancient India, our souls were entirely different from what they are today. They were equipped with entirely different faculties in those ancient times, and lived under wholly different conditions.

And now, so as to fully understand what follows, try to visualize as clearly as possible the nature of our souls after the Atlantean catastrophe—when they were incarnated, let us say, in bodies that could only have existed on earth at that particular time of the ancient Indian civilization. We should not imagine that this civilization was only in India itself, but that in those times the Indian peoples were of prime cultural importance. Forms of civilization differed across the globe, but they all bore the stamp of the teachings which in those times the leaders of humanity gave the peoples of ancient India.

When reflecting on the nature of our souls at that epoch we must realize that in those times it was quite impossible for people to possess the kind of knowledge we do today. There was as yet no awareness of self, no ego-consciousness in the clear, distinct form we find today. A person was scarcely aware that he was an ego. True, the 'I' or ego was already within us as a power or force, but knowledge of this 'I' is not the same thing as its force or activity. Human beings lacked the inward nature they nowadays possess, having instead faculties of a quite different kind, which we have often referred to as ancient, shadowy powers of clairvoyance.

When we study the human soul in those times during its waking life, we find that it did not really experience itself as a distinct ego. Each individual felt himself to be a member of his race or tribe, of his folk. In the sense that the hand is a limb or member of the body, the single 'I' or ego was embodied in the whole community or nation. A person did not feel himself to be an individual 'I' as he does today, but experienced the ego as the folk ego, the tribal ego. During the day he was not really aware of his human nature as such. But when evening came and he fell asleep, his consciousness was not wholly darkened as happens today. During sleep the soul was aware of spiritual realities—for instance of spiritual occurrences in its surroundings of which our dreams today are mere shadows, in most cases no longer conveying their full reality. People had such perceptions at that time and were aware that a world of spirit existed. It was reality for them—not as the result of logical deduction or proof, but because each night, even if in a dim, dreamlike kind of awareness, they actually experienced the world of spirit. But that itself was not the essential thing. As well as sleeping and waking life there were also intermediate states during which people were neither completely asleep nor awake. In such states, ego-consciousness was diminished even more than by day, but perception of spiritual occurrences, this dreamlike clairvoyance, was substantially stronger than at other times during the night. In these intermediate states, therefore, people had no ego conciousness but were clairvoyant—were as if transported and entirely unaware of their separate identity. Rather than knowing himself as a human being, a person felt himself to be an integral part of the world of spirit, the reality of which he beheld. Such were the experiences of human souls in the days of ancient India. And earlier, during the Atlantean epoch, this consciousness, this life in the world of spirit, was even clearer—really a very great deal clearer. We can therefore look back to a time when our souls were endowed with dim, dreamlike clairvoyance which has gradually faded as humanity evolved.

If our souls had remained at this stage of ancient clairvoyance we could not have acquired the individual ego consciousness that we possess today. We could never have been fully aware that we are human beings. We had, so to speak, to exchange our consciousness of the world of spirit for ego or 'I' consciousness. In the future we shall attain a state where both are present together, a state combining clairvoyance in the fullest sense and intact ego consciousness— something that today can only be achieved by someone who undergoes a path of initiation. In the future, though, it will again become possible for everyone to gaze into the world of spirit and yet still to know himself to be a distinct human being, an ego.

Just visualize once again what has occurred. The soul has passed from incarnation to incarnation; once it was clairvoyant, then later on it grew more and more aware of being an ego and was increasingly able to form its own, independent judgements. As long as someone still has clairvoyant vision of the world of spirit and does not feel himself to be an ego, he cannot form judgements, or reason with the intellect. The latter faculty developed steadily, but with every succeeding incarnation the old clairvoyance faded. States in which a person was able to gaze into the world of spirit became rarer as human beings penetrated more and more deeply into the physical world, developing logical thinking and experiencing themselves as egos.

So we can say that in very ancient times we were spiritual beings, for we lived in direct intercourse with other beings of spirit as our companions. We felt a kinship with beings whom we can no longer perceive today with our ordinary senses. Beside the world directly surrounding us there are, as we know, still other worlds peopled by other spiritual beings. With our normal consciousness today we cannot see into these worlds, but in earlier times we lived in them, both during the night-time consciousness of sleep and during the intermediate state I mentioned. We lived within these worlds in communion with these other beings. Normally this is no longer possible for us today. We have been, as it were, cast out of our home, the world of spirit, and with every new incarnation we became more firmly established and rooted in this earthly world.

In the sanctuaries where spiritual life was cultivated, in places of learning and in the fields of study where such things were still known, account was taken of the fact that human beings had incarnated at these different periods of earth's evolution. People still looked back to a very ancient epoch before the Atlantean catastrophe, when human beings lived in direct communion with the gods or beings of spirit, and when their inner life of feeling and sentient experience was naturally quite different. You can imagine, I am sure, that this was so at a time when the soul was fully aware of being able to look upwards to higher beings, and knew itself to be part of that higher world. In considering these things it is worth recalling that we learn to speak and think today by growing up amongst other human beings, through whom alone we can acquire such faculties. If a child were to be placed on some lonely island and grew up without human contact, he would not develop the capacity to speak and think. This shows that the way any being evolves is to some extent dependent on those amongst whom it grows up and lives. We can see this in animals too. It is known that if dogs are removed from the domesticated state where they have contact with human beings to places where they have no such contact, they forget how to bark; as a rule the descendants of such dogs cannot bark at all. So something does depend on the kinds of being surrounding us as we grow up. You can therefore imagine that it is different to live, as a modern soul, among one's contemporaries here on the physical plane than to have lived at an earlier time among beings of spirit in a world of spirit to which normal vision no longer penetrates today. The impulses we develop when living as a human being among human beings are quite different from when we lived among gods.

Higher knowledge has always recognized such things, looking back to that ancient time when people had direct contact with divine beings of spirit. This contact made the soul feel part of the divine world of spirit, and also engendered within it impulses and forces that were still of a divine, spiritual nature—in a quite different sense than we can say of soul forces in our own times. When the soul felt itself to be a part of the higher world, a will spoke out of this soul that also sprang from the divine world of spirit. We can truly say that this was an inspired will because the soul was living closely with the gods.

Higher knowledge speaks of this age, when human beings were still one with divine beings of spirit, as the Golden Age or Krita Yuga.[1] This is a very ancient epoch which preceded the Atlantean catastrophe. Then came an age when people no longer felt their connection with the divine world of spirit so strongly as during Krita Yuga; they no longer felt their impulses were determined by their life with the gods, but their vision of the spirit and soul was already obscured. Nevertheless, they still retained a memory of the time when they dwelt among spiritual beings and the gods.

This memory was still particularly distinct in ancient India. In those times it was very easy to speak of spiritual things. Although one could have directed people's attention then to the external, physically perceptible world, this was still regarded as maya or illusion because such physical perceptions had only recently dawned in human beings. In ancient India, souls no longer beheld the gods themselves but they still perceived spiritual realities and occurrences, and lower-ranking beings of spirit. Only a relatively small number of people could still behold sublime spiritual beings, and even for such people the old, living communion with gods was already much less intense. The will impulses deriving from the divine world of spirit had already faded. Nevertheless, a glimpse into spiritual realities and occurrences was still possible, in certain states of consciousness at any rate: in sleep and in those intermediate states we have mentioned.

The most important aspects of this world of spirit, however, which in former times were experienced as immediate reality, were now present in the form of a kind of knowledge of truth, as something which the soul still knew with certainty but which was now accessible only as knowledge, albeit true. People still lived in the world of spirit, but in this later age awareness of its existence was not as strong as it had once been. This period is called the Silver Age or Treta Yuga.[2]

Then came the period when, upon incarnating, human vision was increasingly sundered from the world of spirit, when our whole nature was directed towards the external sense world and firmly rooted in that world. Inner ego consciousness, human consciousness, became ever more definite and distinct. This is the Bronze Age, or Dvapara Yuga.[3] Human knowledge of the spiritual world was then no longer as sublime or direct as in former times, but something of it at least remained in humanity. This was rather similar to the way, in our own times, people can retain something of the jubilance of youth—it is past and over but it has been known and experienced, and we can speak of it as something we remember. Thus the souls of that age were still to some extent familiar with experiences that directed them towards the worlds of spirit. This was the essential characteristic of Dvapara Yuga.

But then came another age when even this degree of familiarity with the world of spirit ended and the doors of spiritual vision closed. Human attention focused on and was increasingly confined to the external, material world and the intellect which processes sense impressions, so that the only remaining possibility was to ponder on the spiritual world—the least satisfactory way of knowing it. The material and physical world was the real experience people now had. If they wished to know something about the spiritual world they could only do so by thinking or reflecting. This was the age most lacking in spirituality, when human beings fully established themselves in the material world. This was necessary to enable us to gradually develop the highest degree of self-awareness, for only through meeting the strong resistance of the outer world could human beings learn to distinguish themselves from this world and experience themselves as individuals. This age is called Kali Yuga or the Dark Age.[4]

Let me stress that these designations—Krita Yuga for instance—can also be used for longer epochs. Before the Golden Age we experienced and participated in still higher worlds, and so that name could also apply to all those former ages. But if we are happy to take the names as a rough guide to spiritual findings, the periods can be divided as I have described. Specific periods of time can be assigned to all such epochs. While it is true that evolution progresses gradually, there are still certain lines of demarcation before which we can say that certain conditions predominated and, after them, others.

Thus Kali Yuga began approximately in the year 3101 BC. We realize, therefore, that our souls have repeatedly appeared on earth in new incarnations, during which our vision has become increasingly sundered from the spiritual world, becoming ever more confined to the outer world of the senses. We realize, too, that with every incarnation our souls enter into conditions in which there are always new things to learn. In Kali Yuga what we can do is establish and consolidate our ego consciousness—something not possible previously, before we were endowed with ego.

If in a particular incarnation souls fail to absorb what that epoch offers, it is very difficult for the loss to be made good in later epochs. Such souls must wait a long time until the loss can, in some respects, be compensated—but we cannot rely on this compensation occurring.

Let us clearly grasp, therefore, that the closing of the gates to the world of spirit was of fundamental and essential importance. This was also the epoch of John the Baptist, of Christ himself on earth. At that period, when 3100 years of the Dark Age had already elapsed, a fact of salient importance was that all people then alive had already been incarnated several times—once or twice at the very least—in this Dark Age. Ego consciousness had been firmly established; memory of the spiritual realm had faded away, and if people did not wish to lose all connection with the world of spirit it was vital for them to learn to experience the reality of the spiritual world within the ego. The 'I' needed to have developed to the stage where it could be certain, at least in its inmost core, that a world of spirit exists, and likewise higher beings of spirit. The ego needed to have become capable of feeling and believing in the spiritual world.

If at the time of Christ Jesus someone had tried to describe the conditions prevailing then, he might have put it like this: 'In former times people could experience the kingdom of heaven outside of their "I", in those spiritual breadths into which they entered when they went out of themselves. At that time people had to experience the kingdoms of heaven, the world of spirit, at a far remove from the ego. This is no longer possible, for our nature has changed so greatly that these kingdoms must be experienced within the ego itself. The kingdoms of heaven have come so close to human beings that they work right into our "I" or ego.' This, indeed, was what John the Baptist proclaimed when he said: 'The kingdoms of heaven are at hand!' In other words, they have drawn near to the ego. Previously they were outside and beyond us, but now they have drawn close, and we must grasp them in the very core of our being, in the ego. And because in this Dark Age or Kali Yuga human beings could no longer depart from the physical and enter the spiritual world, it was necessary for the divine being, Christ, to descend to the physical world. Christ's descent into a human being of flesh and blood, into Jesus of Nazareth, was necessary so that by beholding

the life and deeds of Christ on the physical plane
people would be able to reconnect, in the physical body, with the kingdoms of heaven, the
spiritual world. And so Christ's sojourn on
earth occurred in the middle of Kali Yuga, the
Dark Age, and those who were not dull and
insensitive but who understood the nature of the
times were able to realize that God's descent to
human beings was necessary to re-establish a
lost connection with the world of spirit.

If no one at the time had been able to find a
living connection with Christ in their hearts and
souls, human beings would gradually have lost
all relationship with spiritual worlds, and
human egos would not have received the kingdom of heaven into themselves. If all who lived
at that crucial point of time had persisted in
darkness, it might well have happened that an
event of such momentous significance would
have passed them by unnoticed. Then human
souls would have withered, wasted and decayed.
True, even without Christ they would have

continued to incarnate for a further period of time, but they would have been unable to implant in the ego the power that enabled them to reconnect with the kingdoms of heaven. The appearance of Christ on earth might have passed completely unnoticed—as it did for example in Rome. At a certain period all that was known of Christ in Rome was the rumour of a strange sect of awful people, living in some filthy street, whom an appalling man calling himself Jesus of Nazareth was inciting to all kinds of villainous deeds! You may also know that the great Roman historian Tacitus wrote in a similar vein about a hundred years after the events in Palestine.

Thus the fact that something of supreme importance had occurred was by no means universally recognized. Few were aware that the divine light had shone into the darkness of earth and that it was therefore possible for human beings to pass safely through the age of Kali Yuga. Humanity's further evolution was assured because certain souls had been on earth at that time who understood the significance of Christ's descent to earth, and knew what was at stake.

If you think yourselves back in time to that period you can realize that it was quite possible to live then without knowing anything at all about Christ's advent on the physical plane. You could easily have lived on earth without any awareness at all of this momentous event.

Today too, surely, something of infinite importance might occur without us being aware of it. Isn't it possible that our contemporaries might fail to have the slightest inkling of the most important occurrence in the world at the present time? Certainly this could happen. Something of supreme importance is indeed taking place, although it is perceptible only to the eyes of spirit.

People talk a great deal about periods of transition; and we ourselves are actually living in a very important one. Its importance lies in the fact that the Dark Age has run its course and a new age is beginning when slowly, gradually, human souls will change and develop new faculties.

The fact that the vast majority of people are entirely unaware of this need not surprise us, for it was the same when the Christ event occurred at the beginning of our era. Kali Yuga came to an end in 1899, and now we need to advance into a new era. New faculties of soul are slowly being prepared in human beings.

The first indications of these new faculties will become noticeable relatively soon in certain, isolated souls; and they will become more apparent in the mid-thirties of this century, roughly between 1930 and 1940. The years 1933, 1935 and 1937 will be particularly important. Very special faculties will start to reveal themselves in human beings as natural gifts. Great changes will take place during this period and biblical prophecies will be fulfilled. Everything will change for souls alive on earth, and also for those no longer incarnated in physical bodies. In whatever realm they dwell, souls are on the way to developing entirely new faculties. Everything is changing; but the supremely important occurrence in our time is a deeply incisive transformation of the faculties of the human soul.

Kali Yuga is over, and human souls are now beginning to develop new faculties. These faculties—since this is the purpose of the new era—will themselves call forth certain powers of clairvoyance which, during Kali Yuga, were inevitably submerged in the unconscious realm. A number of souls will experience the strange condition of having ego consciousness but, at the same time, a sense of living in a world essentially different from the world known to their ordinary consciousness. This experience will be shadowy, like vague apprehension, similar to the experience of someone born blind who undergoes an operation and gains the power to see. What we call esoteric training will

28

be able to help people attain these clairvoyant faculties in a far clearer form. But because human beings progress and evolve anyway, such faculties will also appear in very tentative and elementary form through a natural process of evolution.

It could easily happen, though—indeed far more easily now than at any other time—that people prove unable to grasp these changes which are of such supreme importance for humanity. They might fail to realize that such faculties represent an actual glimpse, though still shadowy and dim, into a world of spirit. There might, for example, be so much wickedness, such entrenched materialism on earth that most people will not show the slightest understanding—instead considering people with this clairvoyance to be lunatics, and shutting them up in asylums with those who really are deranged. This epoch might pass without leaving a trace, although we too are now giving renewed voice to the call of John the Baptist,

Christ's forerunner, and of Christ himself, that a new epoch is at hand when human souls must ascend a step towards the kingdoms of heaven.

This great occurrence might easily pass by without human understanding. If between the years 1930 and 1940 materialists were to utter, triumphantly, that despite a number of fools there has been no sign whatever of the great, expected event, this would not disprove what has been said in the slightest. But if materialism were to prevail and humanity entirely overlooked these occurrences, it would be a dire misfortune. Even if people prove incapable of perceiving them, great things will come to pass.

One of these is that it will become possible for people to acquire a new faculty of perceiving the etheric world—a few to start with, followed by ever-increasing numbers, for humanity will have 2500 years during which to develop and perfect these faculties. This opportunity must not be missed. If it were, this would be a tragic misfortune and humanity would have to wait until a later epoch to make good the lost opportunity, and at last develop this new faculty. It will involve people growing able to see in their surroundings something of the etheric world which previously they have not normally been able to perceive. Today human beings see only the human physical body, but then they will become able to see the etheric body at least as a shadowy formation, and also to perceive the connection between profounder occurrences in the etheric world. They will perceive images and premonitions of occurrences in the world of spirit, and find that after three or four days such events then occur on the physical plane. We will see certain things in etheric images and know that next day, or in a few days' time, this or that will occur.

The faculties of the human soul will be transformed. And what is associated with this? The being whom we call Christ once walked the earth in flesh and blood at the beginning of our era. He will never again return in a physical body, for that was a unique event and will not be repeated. But he will come again in an etheric form in the period I have mentioned. People will learn to perceive Christ by virtue of growing towards him through this etheric perception. He will not now descend as far as the physical body but only as far as the etheric. Human beings must therefore grow to the stage where he can be perceived, for Christ spoke truly when he said: 'I am with you always, even unto the end of the days of earth.' He is present in our spiritual world, and those especially blessed can always see him in this spiritual, etheric world.

Paul in his vision at Damascus was someone who gained particularly intense conviction by means of such perception. But this etheric vision will develop in individual human beings as a natural faculty. In the future it will become increasingly possible for people to experience what Paul experienced at Damascus.

We can now grasp a quite different aspect of spiritual science, realizing that it prepares us for an actual event, the reappearance of the Christ. Christ will appear again inasmuch as human beings raise themselves up to him with their etheric vision. When we understand this then spiritual science is seen to be the means to prepare us to perceive Christ's return. By rendering us mature enough to grasp this great event of Christ's second coming, spiritual science helps us avoid the misfortune of overlooking it. People will become able to see etheric bodies, and among these also the etheric body of Christ. In other words, they will grow into a world where Christ is revealed to their newly awoken faculties.

It will then no longer be necessary to compile all kinds of documentary evidence to prove Christ's existence, for eyewitnesses will testify to the living presence of Christ, perceiving him in his etheric body. This experience will tell them that this being is the same who fulfilled the Mystery of Golgotha at the beginning of our era, and that he is indeed the Christ. Just as Paul at

Damascus was utterly sure at the time that he perceived the Christ, so there will be human beings whose experiences in the etheric world will persuade and assure them that Christ truly lives.

The true nature of the second coming of Christ is the supreme mystery of the age in which we now live. But the materialistic mind will in a certain sense appropriate this event. What I have said—that all true spiritual knowledge points to the importance of this age—will often be proclaimed in the years to come. But the materialistic mind corrupts everything nowadays, and such thinking will be quite incapable of grasping that human souls must advance to the stage of etheric vision and thus to vision of Christ in the etheric body.

Materialistic thinking will conceive this event as a descent of Christ in the flesh, a physical incarnation. In boundless arrogance, a number of people will turn this to their own advantage and present themselves to the world as the reincarnated Christ. The near future may therefore bring false Christs, but anthroposophists should be so fully prepared for the spiritual life that they do not confuse the return of the Christ in a spiritual body, perceptible only to higher vision, with a return in a physical body of flesh and blood. This will be one of the worst temptations besetting humanity. To lead people beyond this will be the task of those who learn through spiritual science to rise to true understanding of the spirit; who, rather than trying to drag spirit down to matter, seek to ascend into the world of spirit themselves. It is in this sense that we can speak of the return of Christ and of the fact that we rise to Christ in the spiritual world through acquiring the faculty of etheric vision.

Christ is always and everywhere present, but he is in the world of spirit. We can reach him when we rise into that world. All anthroposophical teaching should be transformed within us into an indomitable will not to allow this occurrence to pass unnoticed but, in the time that remains to us, to gradually enable humanity to develop these new faculties and thus to reunite with Christ. Otherwise humanity would have to wait ages before such an opportunity could come again, would have to wait in fact for a new incarnation of the earth itself. If this event of Christ's return were overlooked, vision of Christ in the etheric body would be limited to those willing to fit themselves for such an experience through esoteric training. But the really momentous change whereby humanity in general, all human beings, could acquire these faculties and understand this great event by means of them would be impossible for long, long ages.

It is evident therefore that the very nature of our age justifies the existence and work of spiritual science in the world. It does not aim merely to satisfy theoretical demands or academic curiosity. The aim of spiritual science is to prepare people for this great event, for their rightful place in the epoch in which they live, so that with clear understanding and knowledge they perceive what is actually present but might otherwise pass us by without coming to fruition.

It will be of the utmost importance to recognize and understand this event of Christ's appearance, for it will be followed by other events. Just as other occurrences preceded the Christ event in Palestine, so after the time I have referred to—after he himself has become visible to humanity again in the etheric body—those who foretold his coming will follow his reappearance. Those who prepared his coming will be recognizable in a new form to people who experience the new Christ event. Those who lived on earth as Moses, Abraham and the Prophets will be recognizable once again. And it will become clear that just as Abraham preceded Christ and prepared the way for him, so, after Christ's advent, his mission likewise will be to help in his work. Someone therefore who does not just sleep through the forthcoming event of supreme importance will find his way into glad fellowship and fraternity with all those who, as the Patriarchs, preceded the Christ event. The whole choir will be revealed of those to whose level we shall thus be able to rise. The one who led humanity downwards to the physical plane will reappear after Christ and lead us upwards again, uniting us once more with spiritual worlds.[5]

Looking far back into the past we arrive at the moment in humanity's evolution when humanity starts to leave the worlds of spirit behind and descend ever further into the physical world. Although the following image also has its material aspect, we can still use it here. In former times we were the companions of spiritual beings; and because our spirit lived in the world of spirit, we were a son of the gods. But the soul, descending ever more deeply into physical incarnation, participated increasingly in the external world. The son of gods in us took delight, we may say, in the daughters of earth— that is, our souls were drawn to the physical world. This means, in turn, that in earlier times the human spirit was entirely immersed in divine spirituality, but then sank down into physical materiality, espousing brain-bound intellect, and becoming entangled through it in the physical world's sensory web. And now the human spirit must reascend on the path by which it once descended, to become once more a son of the gods. The human spirit which became the son of man would perish in the physical world if this son of man were not to climb upwards again to the divine beings, to the light of the spiritual world, finding delight in future in the daughters of the gods. For humanity's evolution it was necessary that the sons of the gods should unite with the daughters of men, with souls fettered to the earth, so that, as the son of man, the human spirit could learn to master the physical plane. But now the human being of the future, the son of man, should delight in the daughters of the gods—in the divine, spiritual light of wisdom with which he must reunite so as to grow upwards again into the world of the gods.

The human will must be fired by divine wisdom, and the most powerful impetus for this will be if those who have truly prepared themselves begin to perceive the sublime etheric form of Christ Jesus. To someone in whom natural clairvoyance has developed, this will be like a second coming of Christ Jesus, just as the etheric Christ appeared as a spiritual being to Paul. Christ will once again appear to human beings when they realize that they must, for this purpose, use the faculties which evolution will develop in the human soul.

Let us therefore use spiritual science not merely to satisfy our intellectual curiosity but in a way that makes us worthier to fulfil the great tasks and missions of the human race.

Answer by Rudolf Steiner to questions asked after the lecture:

When light is cast, as today, on mysteries of a more subtle and sensitive nature, let us not treat them as thoughtlessly as people are apt to treat certain subjects nowadays. Instead let us realize that anthroposophy must be altogether different from theory. Its insights have to be taught—for how could one rise to the kinds of ideas presented today if not in the form of teaching? The essence of this teaching, however, is that it does not remain a mere doctrine but is reforged in the soul into qualities of heart and character, into an entirely different attitude of mind, and changes us as human beings. The teachings presented here should guide us in making the best use of our incarnations, so that through them we can develop new and quite different attributes.

I have tried not to say a word too many or too few, and have therefore only fleetingly referred to matters of great moment. But what has been said is significant not only for souls who will incarnate in the period between 1930 and 1940 but also for those who at that time will dwell in the world of spirit between death and a new birth. Souls work down from the spiritual world into the world of those living on earth, even though the latter know nothing about this. Through the Christ event this communion between souls incarnated here on the physical plane and those already in the spiritual world will become increasingly conscious. Active cooperation between incarnated human beings and spiritual beings will then be possible. I meant to indicate this when I said that the Prophets will appear again among human beings on earth.

You should therefore see it like this. When these great times arrive in the future, more conscious cooperation will come about between human beings in the physical world and in the spiritual world. This is not possible today because of the lack of a common language. Here in the physical world the only words human beings use in their languages denote physical things and conditions. The world in which human beings live between death and a new birth is quite different from the world that directly surrounds us, and they speak a different language. The dead can absorb only what is spoken here that relates to spiritual science—nothing else. In anthroposophy we are therefore cultivating something that will be increasingly intelligible to the dead, to those living in worlds of spirit between death and a new birth.

Humanity is entering a new era when influences proceeding from the spiritual world will steadily increase in intensity. The great events of the immediate future will be perceptible in all worlds. Those too who are living between death and a new birth will have new experiences resulting from the new Christ event in the etheric world. But if they have made no preparation for them while on earth, they will no more understand this event than will people in physical incarnation who have not prepared themselves in the right way. It is vital for all souls now incarnated—no matter whether they will still be in physical incarnation then or not—to prepare themselves for these important events by assimilating anthroposophical insights. If they fail to receive into their earthly consciousness what anthroposophy or spiritual science has to offer, they will have to wait for a new incarnation to have an opportunity here on earth of absorbing the relevant teachings. There are indeed things that can only be experienced and learned on earth.

This is why we say, for example, that death cannot be known in the spiritual world, and that for a God to die he had to descend into the physical world. Understanding of the Mystery of Golgotha can be acquired only in the way that is possible in the physical world. We have been led down into the physical world to acquire something that can only be acquired here. And Christ descended to humanity because it was only in the physical world that he could reveal to human beings—could enable them to experience in the Mystery of Golgotha—something whose fruits ripen and endure in the spiritual world but whose seeds must be sown here in the physical world.

Notes

The text is a record of a lecture Rudolf Steiner gave to members of the Anthroposophical Society in Karlsruhe on 25 January 1910.

1. The Krita Yuga lasted about 20,000 years.
2. The Treta Yuga lasted about 15,000 years.
3. The Dvapara Yuga lasted about 10,000 years.
4. The Kali Yuga lasted about 5,000 years (from 3101 BC to AD 1899). Our current age will continue for a further 2,500 years.
5. See the lecture Steiner gave on 6 March 1910 in *The Reappearance of Christ in the Etheric* (SteinerBooks, 2003).

Further Reading

Rudolf Steiner's fundamental books:

Knowledge of the Higher Worlds
also published as: *How to Know Higher Worlds*

Occult Science
also published as: *An Outline of Esoteric Science*

Theosophy

The Philosophy of Freedom
also published as: *Intuitive Thinking as a
Spiritual Path*

Some relevant volumes of Rudolf Steiner's lectures:

The Christian Mystery
From Jesus to Christ
Christ and the Human Soul
The Fifth Gospel
Rosicrucian Wisdom
Founding a Science of the Spirit

For all titles contact Rudolf Steiner Press (UK) or
SteinerBooks (USA):
www.rudolfsteinerpress.com www.steinerbooks.org

Publisher's Note on
Rudolf Steiner's Lectures

The lecture contained in this volume has been translated from the German, which is based on stenographic and other recorded texts that were in most cases never seen or revised by the lecturer. Hence, due to human errors in hearing and transcription, they may contain mistakes and faulty passages. Every effort has been made to ensure that this is not the case. Some of Steiner's lectures were given to audiences more familiar with anthroposophy; these are the so-called 'private' or 'members' lectures. Other lectures, like the written works, were intended for the general public. The difference between these, as Rudolf Steiner indicates in his *Autobiography*, is twofold. On the one hand, the members' lectures take for granted a background in and commitment to anthroposophy; in the public lectures this was not the case. At the same time, the members' lectures address the concerns and dilemmas of the members, while the public work speaks directly out of Steiner's own understanding of universal needs. Nevertheless, as Rudolf Steiner stresses: 'Nothing was ever said that was not solely the result of my direct experience of the growing content of anthroposophy. There was never any question of concessions to the prejudices and preferences of the members. Whoever reads these privately printed lectures can take them to represent anthroposophy in the fullest sense. Thus it was possible without hesitation—when the complaints in this direction became too persistent—to depart from the custom of circulating this material "For members only". But it must be borne in mind that faulty passages do occur in these reports not revised by myself.' Earlier in the same chapter, he states: 'Had I been able to correct them [*the private lectures*], the restriction *for members only* would have been unnecessary from the beginning.'

Other budget-priced volumes from Rudolf Steiner Press

Single lectures:
The Dead Are With Us
Educating Children Today
An Exercise for Karmic Insight
The Four Temperaments
How Can I Find the Christ?
How to Cure Nervousness
The Work of the Angel in Our Astral Body

Meditations:
Breathing the Spirit, Meditations for Times of Day &
Seasons of the Year
Calendar of the Soul, The Year Participated
The Foundation Stone Meditation